BLACK AND WHITE:

How to Have Our American Conversation About Race

DAVID EVANS

Cover Design: Fahnestock Landgar

ISBN: 978-0-929422-94-7

CONTENTS

CHAPTER 1: HOW TO HAVE OUR AMERICAN CONVERSATION ABOUT RACE 1

CHAPTER 2: THE ELEPHANT IN AMERICA'S LIVING ROOM: SLAVERY 10

CHAPTER 3: HOW DO YOU DEFINE RACISM? 15

CHAPTER 4: A JUSTICE TITHE 20

CHAPTER 5: IS THERE JUSTICE IN AMERICA? 24

CHAPTER 6: THE SECOND ASSASSINATION OF MARTIN LUTHER KING 29

CHAPTER 7: THE DECLARATION OF INDEPENDENCE, PART 2 33

CHAPTER 8: "WE HAVE MET THE ENEMY AND IT IS US" 38

ABOUT THE AUTHOR 49

CHAPTER 1

HOW TO HAVE OUR AMERICAN CONVERSATION ABOUT RACE

An unarmed young Black man is gunned down by a white policeman, and, in the outcry that follows, someone, usually a white person, always says, "We need to have a conversation." But somehow that conversation never seems to happen.

Then the cycle is repeated in some other city, and once again we hear the familiar refrain, "We need to have a conversation."

We desperately ***do*** need to have a conversation. But where? And how?

I believe I've found an answer to these questions. Several years ago, I accidentally stumbled onto a situation that provides a key for having that national conversation. It's a kind of template. I've tried it out locally and had excellent results. And it could be replicated across the country.

Here's what happened:

In 1992 in Los Angeles a young Black man named Rodney King was stopped by the police and savagely beaten. A bystander happened to take a video of the beating and the video went viral. People around the world were outraged, and the police responsible for the beating were brought to trial.

But at the conclusion of the trial the police were acquitted of wrongdoing, and a huge swath of the city exploded in a fury of outrage and flames.

Predictably, key spokesmen for the city and the white community responded by saying, "We need to have a conversation."

At the time, I was going to an almost completely white church on the west side of Los Angeles. (I myself am white.) One of the pastors there knew a minister in a Black church in South Los Angeles, and they set up some exchanges between the two churches. We had a couple of meetings, but the relationship never went very far, and the two churches drifted back into their separate demographics.

But during those two meetings, I met a Black woman who invited me to attend her Black church. So, I went.

I had a great deal of trepidation about going into such a dangerous part of the city. It was adjacent to the very area that had recently been engulfed in flames and rebellion.

But at the same time, I was very conscious that there is a huge, historic problem between the Black and white races in this country. And, as individuals, each of us is either part of the problem or part of the solution.

I wanted to be part of the solution.

At that point, I had no real "strategy," no plan, and no agenda. And I had no relevant skills or training. At that time in my life all I had ever done was write, and what I'd written almost entirely was comedy. (I wrote for "The Monkees" TV show, and "Love American Style," among other things.)

But I felt I needed to do something. And when you don't know what else to do, at least you can show up. So, I showed up.

I was the only white person in a sea of Black faces.

It so happens that the times of the Sunday services, and also the locations of the Black and white churches, were such that I could often go to both churches on the same Sunday. So, I began going to the Black church, and I also continued going to my original white church.

It was a lot of church every Sunday! But it worked. (I grew up as the son of a Presbyterian minister, so I was "churchified" at an early age.)

Many people in my white church initially seemed very interested and enthusiastic about my "experiment." I invited people to come join me, and a couple did once or twice.

But when people began to see that I was really serious about continuing in the Black church, their attitude changed slightly. It wasn't a huge, dramatic change, but it was nonetheless quite discernable. People seemed a little uncomfortable with what I was doing, and weren't quite sure what to make of it, or how to respond.

But I got a very different response in the Black church.

One Sunday after I'd been there about six months, the pastor announced that one of the men in the congregation had received an award for some good works he had recently done. (I forget now exactly what it was; I just remember being impressed.)

At the coffee hour later, I congratulated him, and in the middle of my comments, he just stopped and gave me a long, thoughtful look. Then he said, "You're really here, aren't you?" And I said, "Yes, I am."

It was a very quiet moment, but was extremely profound.

What he was referring to was a common phenomenon I have observed many times. White people will come, expressing great enthusiasm for the church. But they never seem to stay. Two white women appeared once from another Presbyterian church, proclaiming their intention of having their church form a "sister-church relationship" with our Black church. They seemed quite excited by the prospect.

They came for three Sundays and then vanished. That was ten years ago.

So, when the young man I complimented that Sunday commented that "I was really *here*," his comment occurred in a large and meaningful context.

Somewhere along the way, I became aware that there was one particular question that everyone in the white church always asked me. And not just one or two people, but ***everyone!*** And the question was this:

"How have they treated you?"

The answer is really very simple: they've treated me wonderfully well! My time at the Black church has been an amazing blessing. I have made many friends there, and it is one of the joyous high points of my life.

I have a theory about this. Black people have experienced so much rejection and resistance in so many ways from white people, both consciously and unconsciously, that they are really delighted when a white person shows that he or she truly values and appreciates them. On *their* turf!

"How have they treated you?"

I return to this question often. The fact that virtually every white person asked me this same question shows dramatically what a gigantic chasm there is between white people and Black people in this country. White people generally have no idea about the real lives of Black people.

Why not?

The reason is that, although many of the bastions of segregation have long ago fallen or have disappeared, the Black and white races still remain very separated.

In fact, a recent Reuters/Ipsos poll found that, among white Americans, 40% are surrounded exclusively by white friends. So inevitably they're cut off from the perspectives of Black people. They have no idea about the real state of race relations in the United States.

And, although the majority of Black people I know agree that there have been amazing improvements in race relations in America in the last fifty years, many feel that there is still a stubborn core of racism in our country. But most white people are completely oblivious to that viewpoint.

During my twenty-five years in the Black church I have had many joyful experiences and life highpoints. But a number of friends there have also shared personal stories of pain and exclusion.

I have a young Black friend who is extremely intelligent, college and seminary educated, and is now a minister. He shared with me once about how painful it is for him to walk down a street and experience the palpable fear and resistance that white people radiate when they see him coming. They often cross the street just to avoid him.

They don't see a person who might be intelligent, sensitive, or compassionate. They just see a person who is Black, and somehow "other" or "the enemy," and they reflexively give in to that negative, fear response. My friend told me that this scenario occurs frequently and crushes his spirit.

What should we do?

I believe one of the most important things we need to do in our country today is to find ways to help white people understand the depth of the pain and struggle that Black people have gone through, and continue to go through in America. We need to have that conversation, so that white people in this country can hear and finally understand what's really going on in American race relations.

I believe that my experience of going to a Black church for a number of years helps provide a model for a framework within which a powerful, authentic and transformative conversation about race can take place. Here are some principles and guidelines that I believe can insure the success of that conversation:

- **White people need to take the initiative for "the conversation about race."** Our race started the whole problem with the institution of slavery, so we need to take the initiative in helping to improve the situation.
- **It is important to make a personal long-term commitment to this project.** It takes a big commitment, because we are addressing a deep, long-term problem that has defined much of our American history and still does. It *requires* a big commitment.
- **Don't start off by focusing on trying to have "a conversation about race." Instead, focus on building deep, honest, authentic friendships that bless all participants.** Then let any "conversation about race" flow naturally and organically out of these friendships. Don't force it. Be patient and accepting.

When I began going to my Black church this was the course I instinctively followed. I just started getting to know people and entered into the life of the church.

One thing I did was to join the Gospel Choir. It was a wonderful experience, was very bonding, and became the basis for many deep friendships. And it was some of the best Gospel/jazz/blues music I've ever heard! (I am a jazz enthusiast.)

The result was not so much one big, definitive, analytical conversation, summarizing the state of race relations in America. Instead, what followed was a host of spontaneous connections, blazing like fireflies in the night sky, personal conversations, deep and wonderful, where we shared and recognized one another's fragile humanity in our astonishing mutual enterprise of life.

- **I believe that for the conversation about race to be most successful, it is very valuable for white people to be in the minority.** There are a couple of reasons for this.

One is that, if you're a white person and are almost always in the majority, then inevitably you get a very distorted and limited view of life and the human condition. Lots of other people are in minority situations most of the time. It's good for white people to share the experience of that reality.

Another reason is that for Black people, situations where whites are in the majority can often create uneasiness and feelings of being judged. I believe Black people feel much freer and are able to act with much greater authenticity when they're in the majority.

So, I believe that situations with Blacks in the majority are good for **both** white people and Black people.

- **I believe the "conversation about race" can happen best in a church community.**

Twenty-five years ago, when I began my adventure in expanded race relations, I began it in a church. It just seemed intuitively right.

And as time has gone on that choice seems even more right than it did then.

One great thing about churches in the same denomination is that they exist in a wide variety of very different communities. But they all share some remarkably similar structures and traditions. I could go from a Presbyterian church in a white community, to a Presbyterian church near where the riots occurred, with two totally different congregations racially. Yet they were both very similar in their ecclesiastical structure, traditions and practices. They were both very recognizably Presbyterian.

So, in my radical adventure to move into a different racial group, it was very helpful that both groups of people shared the same organizational framework. This is sort of like pivoting in basketball: one foot moves all around, but the other foot stays in the same place without moving. (That's the "Presbyterian foot.")

Another great thing about having a church as the setting for my adventure in expanded race relations, is that my personal adventure aligned with one of the great missions of the church: to bring people together in harmony, and to recognize our mutual humanity as fellow children of God.

So, this is the story of the grand racial adventure I've been involved in for the last twenty-five years. It has been one of the greatest experiences of my life. It has, of course, been deeply personal. But as it has unfolded, I have become aware that what I was experiencing was also a template for a clearly defined process that could be repeated by thousands of other people in churches (and also Jewish people from temples) all across the country.

It is a template that shows us how we can finally have that "conversation about race." It won't be some oracular mega conversation, but will be a multitude of mini conversations that blossom up along the way in authentic relationships between friends.

So, yes, we need to have a conversation about race.

And there is a definite template that shows us how we can have this conversation. I encourage everyone to begin this adventure! It is wonderful and transformative. And if enough of us made this journey, I believe we could change the world.

We need to have a conversation.

XXX

CHAPTER 2

THE ELEPHANT IN AMERICA'S LIVING ROOM: SLAVERY

Have you talked about slavery lately?

If you are white, your answer to this question is probably, "no." You not only haven't talked about slavery lately, you may never have talked about it. After all, The Emancipation Proclamation was signed in 1863. Slavery is ancient history. The country has moved on.

Or has it?

For Black people the answer to the question of talking about slavery is often quite different. Slavery is the most defining feature of life in America for Black people. And though Black people were emancipated from the practice of overt chattel slavery, they haven't been emancipated from the long-term consequences of slavery, which continue today. They talk about slavery and process it often.

I've had the opportunity of witnessing these two different viewpoints toward slavery at close hand because, for the last twenty-five years, I have been going concurrently to two different churches, one Black and the other white. There is no single topic that divides these two groups of people more dramatically than the topic of slavery.

Black people are acutely aware that many of the attitudes and practices toward Black people that started during slavery became so entrenched that they continued long afterward, even to the present day. One of these is the enforced separation of the two races, first through slavery itself, then later through segregation.

But other aspects of slavery were even more insidious than physically enforced separation. In order for slaveholders to enforce their authority over slaves, they treated them as inferiors, disempowering them by mistreatment, breaking up Black families by selling off individual family members to other slaveholders, and by making it illegal for Blacks to learn to read.

There has been enormous progress in recent decades. Nonetheless, racism continues. Many of the Black people I know feel that, in spite of all the progress that has been made, America is still a racist country. And, in a sermon I recently heard, the Black preacher called the country to a new level of honesty and accountability. "America can never be healed," he said, "until we first deal with the question of slavery."

But the very topic is radioactive and taboo for many white people.

Since the main feature of slavery was the subjugation of Black people by white people, often through great cruelty, it is an extremely uncomfortable topic for whites. It is hushed into non-existence either through denial or active avoidance. Slavery is the elephant in white America's living room.

We are at an impasse in this discussion, and in many ways, it is like a classic dispute. I believe my own professional experience can help here.

For the last twenty years I've been actively involved in the field of conflict resolution, and for five years was a court appointed mediator in the Los Angeles Superior Court.

I've worked on a huge variety of different cases: couples splitting up, business conflicts, neighborhood and real-estate disagreements, family and custody issues, organization problems, and contract disputes.

Each case is unique, and they are wildly different from one another. Still, in spite of that, there is one theme that runs through almost all the cases. Time and again the aggrieved party, the one who has been wronged, feels they haven't been ***heard.*** They feel the other party hasn't listened to them.

This is exactly the situation we have with Black people, white people and slavery.

Slavery exerts such a huge and continuing influence over the lives of Black people, that they frequently revisit it and process it. And they feel a great need for white people to acknowledge the reality of slavery, and recognize that, because of its legacy, Black people and white people are born into very different worlds, with very different challenges and advantages. These things are hugely important to Black people and they want white people to verbally acknowledge them.

Black people want to be heard. They need to be listened to.

But all too often white people react with denial and indifference. They respond to the painful history of Black America and slavery with passive-aggressive silence.

Is it possible to move beyond this impasse?

I believe it is.

When I began going to a Black church twenty-five years ago I stumbled into a situation that provides a wonderful opportunity for Black people and white people to talk about slavery in an atmosphere of friendship and mutual respect.

My time at the Black church has been an amazing, joyful, and transforming experience! By developing close friendships with Black people, I have had the opportunity of having many conversations about slavery and related issues. The experience has been one of the greatest blessings of my life.

I realize also that the experience I have had as a white person going to a Black church, provides a kind of template, that could be followed by any number of people across the country. It is a way we could begin to bring about the racial healing we so desperately need.

I recommend it highly! The experience can be a huge blessing. I know it has been for me.

For a white person going to a Black church, it is important not to try to initially force an awkward "conversation about race." Instead, just focus on building deep, honest, authentic friendships that bless all participants. Any conversation about race or slavery should flow naturally and organically out of these friendships. It may take quite a while. That's fine. Don't force it. Be patient and accepting.

For many white people, the idea of going to a Black church, in a different neighborhood, where they will be in the minority is un-nerving, and maybe even fearful. I know it was for me at first, until I realized what a resounding welcome I would receive.

So, there is an elephant in America's living room: slavery. And we all need to talk about it. Black people need to be **heard**. And white people need to **listen.**

It's time to begin.

XXX

CHAPTER 3

HOW DO YOU DEFINE RACISM?

The two churches I have been going to for the last twenty-five years, one Black and one white, have many similarities. They are both churches, and they are both in the same Presbyterian denomination. So, there are ecclesiastical commonalities. But there are certain topics where the viewpoints between the two congregations are completely different. A big one is racism.

If you were to ask people in the white church if they feel that we live in a racist country, almost all of them would confidently say, "No." (I have, in fact, asked a number of people this question.) But if you were to ask Black people that same question, "Is America a racist country?" my experience is that most of them would say, "Yes, it is."

So what exactly *is* racism?

Many white people think of racism historically and geographically. It occurred before the sixties, mostly in the Deep South, and is personified by the Ku Klux

Klan and the archetypal Bull Conner and his snarling dogs. But with the advent of national television, such egregious displays caused great public outcry, so, for a long time they were much less frequent.

In more recent times however, there has been a resurgence of overt racial hostility, with shootings of young Black men by police, and public demonstrations by neo Nazis and allied organizations.

But, in addition to such visible displays, racism also plays out in a multitude of smaller, less obvious ways. And these are some of the most profound.

For example, a Black woman I know told me she was recently in the drugstore standing in line to be waited on. A white man came in after her, and the clerk started to wait on him first, completely ignoring her!

My friend found this a very hurtful, racist experience, and one that is far too typical. It plays out over and over again with endless variations.

Another woman I know works at a local university, and frequently stands at the front counter in the department office to answer questions from students. She is Black. She said that whenever there are two people answering questions at the counter, and the other person is white, students **always** go to the white person first in preference to her.

Still another friend, also a Black woman, told me that she was walking down a hallway in a building recently when an elderly white woman ahead of her stumbled and fell. When my friend rushed over to help her up, the woman angrily refused her help, as though my friend were trying to attack her.

These incidents all felt very racist to the people that experienced them. In typical racist experiences, Black people say they are either treated as invisible, they are devalued, or they are feared.

None of these incidents I just mentioned are by themselves overly dramatic. You wouldn't see them on the front page of the newspaper or the evening news. But when they occur as often and as widely as they do, they create a very negative climate for Black people. So, for them, America often feels like a very racist country.

But as powerful and omnipresent as these racist experiences are for Blacks, they are largely invisible to white people. What can we do to remedy this painful imbalance?

I believe each of these incidents is caused by the simple fact that white people often don't know any Black people or have friendships with them. I return to the Reuters/Ipsos poll I mentioned in chapter one. In this poll, 40% of white people said that their friends are all other whites, and that they don't have any friends of other races.

This is an amazing statistic! It indicates that a huge number of white people don't know any Black people, and consequently have no basis for knowing what Black people are really like. They are operating from ignorance, and often end up acting in very inappropriate and hurtful ways. Inevitably a lot of things they do are quite racist and they don't even know it.

Is it possible to resolve these two very dissonant views of racism?

I believe it is. Looking again at those incidents that my Black friends related to me, they all involved white people engaged in actions that felt very racist to the Black people. But I don't personally believe that the white people did them with malicious intent. I believe they acted thoughtlessly, without even being aware of what they were doing.

And that gets back to the earlier statistic from the Reuters/Ipsos poll, showing that 40% of white don't have any friendships with Black people or other people of color. I believe that if more white people from that 40% group were open to developing some authentic, long-term, caring, equal friendships with Black people, they would be much less likely to engage in thoughtless, racist behavior.

And, as I have mentioned earlier, I believe that the best place to begin to forge those authentic, long-term, caring friendships with Black people is for white people to go to a Black church on a long-term basis. I believe that's where it can happen best.

Why should white people go to a Black church? First of all, because, when things are working right, churches can be very optimistic places, where good positive relationships are encouraged, both with God and with other people.

And secondly it is important that it be a **Black** church, where you as a white person are in the minority. When Blacks are in the majority, my experience is that they are much more likely to be open and honest. You'll probably hear a lot more truth.

But if that same Black person you heard truth from in a Black church, were to be in a white church, he or she would now be in a situation that mirrors the ones he normally encounters in general society, where he often experiences racism. So, there is likely to be a lot less openness and a lot less truth.

Still another reason for a white person to go to a Black church is for the opportunity of being in the minority. Since white people are so numerically dominant in most of America, we get used to that situation, and it creates some unquestioned assumptions about the nature of things and the "rightness" and "appropriateness" of that dominance. So, for a white person to be in a Black church can be a wonderfully humbling and clarifying experience. Skin color aside, things just look different when you're in the minority.

So for these reasons, I believe the transformative journey to racial understanding can happen best in a Black church, where we, as white people are in the minority. And I believe that if white people were to become involved in a Black church, they'd have a much deeper and clearer understanding of the true nature of racism in America. And we could begin to bring about some great and powerful healing in our country.

We could do it.

Let us begin!

XXX

CHAPTER 4

A JUSTICE TITHE

We are born into different Americas. Black people, though freed from the formal constraints of slavery, are nonetheless weighted down by the gravitational pull of its legacy.

But whites are born into a very different America. Relative to Black people, they are born into an America with much greater freedom, acceptance, opportunity, access and education. It is an America of Privilege.

The United States is an economic powerhouse. But it was the work of unpaid slaves that provided the foundation for much of that prosperity.

In 1836, nearly half of all the economic activity in the United States, $600 million dollars, was derived directly or indirectly from the cotton produced by the country's one million slaves.

(For an excellent account of the economic history of the United States, see "The Half That Has Never Been

Told: Slavery and the Making of American Capitalism," by Edward E. Baptist.)

How can our country, and white people in particular, ever repay this enormous debt for the sinful injustice of slavery?

A strategy that has been suggested is to pay reparations in some way to Black people. And in "Atlantic" magazine, Ta Na-Hisi Coates has made an eloquent and persuasive case for reparations.

I personally believe very strongly in the moral rightness of paying reparations to Black people. But how would it work? How would the mechanics of such a program be implemented?

I believe a reparations program would have its greatest effectiveness if it came in some way from the federal government. But our current political divisions around issues of race and ethnicity make that almost impossible. So, let me suggest another alternative:

I propose that white people, as individuals, or as members of groups, voluntarily contribute **A Justice Tithe** to Black people and organizations.

The concept of the "tithe" is one that comes to us from the practices of Christianity and Judaism. People in these traditions typically take a tenth of all the money and worldly goods they receive during any particular period of time, and return it to God. This is done in thanksgiving for all the gifts we have received. Indeed, even for the gift of life itself! But it is also done to help continue the work of the church or synagogue, whatever that might be.

I would like to propose that those of us who are white take the model of the tithe and extend it into the more secular realm of society and racial relations.

We would donate it to Black people in *gratitude* for their substantial contribution as a race to the spiritual and economic foundation of this country. America is a great country, and it is so, in large part because of the presence and spirit of Black people.

I envision A Justice Tithe as an individual contribution that people could make, on a regular basis, out of their own personal resources (money, time or talents) not only to show gratitude, but also, in specific ways, to help better the lives of Black people in America.

As for places to make our Justice Tithe contributions, I believe one of the best ways we could help improve the lives of Black people in America, is by helping to improve their educational opportunities.

Dr. Robert Ross, CEO of the California Endowment, published a recent article in the *Los Angeles Times*, titled, *"Boosting Young Men of Color."* In it he cited an incredible statistic. He said that, of all the young African American males born in this country, fully a third will spend time in prison or in jail. A third!

Dr. Ross goes on to mention three early predictors that young boys are heading toward prison. They are:

Suspensions and early truancy from school. Either of these factors occurring in a young boy's life increases the likelihood he will drop out.

Justice system involvement. Any involvement a young person has with the justice system is more likely to get worse than it is to get better.

Third grade reading level. Dr. Ross says that students who are unable to read proficiently by third grade, are four times more likely to drop out before graduation. And that fully 80% of young, third-grade Black boys are unable to read at grade level!

So, I propose that, for A Justice Tithe, we focus on helping young Black boys improve their reading skills and their schoolwork. Here are three ways we could do that:

- **One-on-One Mentoring.** There are many situations where one-on-one mentoring has made a crucial difference in some young person's life. It is especially important for young boys to have an adult male in their lives, to help them, guide them, and provide an on-going role model to encourage good reading practices. One-on-one mentoring can redeem lives that might otherwise be lost.

• **Group Mentoring and Tutoring**. I recently heard about a group mentoring and tutoring program that was started in an inner-city church. It was designed to help the young people in the neighborhood and is working very successfully. There are three adults that serve as mentors, and they work with about twelve kids from the neighborhood. They meet once a week, have a meal together, and provide a great oasis of support for the kids. One of the key emphases of this program is an emphasis on reading skill.

• **Reading Aloud to Young Children**. One of the single most valuable things adults can do for young children is to read aloud to them. Being read aloud to as a child is a great predictor of success in later life. Hearing wonderful stories broadens children's understanding and enlarges their universe. The experience also helps them develop the language skills they will need to draw on later, no matter what they do.

So here are three things we could do for A Justice Tithe. They are things any of us could do, they are very **do**-able, and they could potentially have an extremely positive, transformative effect.

Although there has been much progress in race relations in America, there is an enormous amount that still needs to be done.

A Justice Tithe could help.

XXX

CHAPTER 5

IS THERE JUSTICE IN AMERICA?

Spending time in my Black church has sensitized me to many issues in the Black experience that I wasn't aware of before. A big one is the issue of mass incarceration. And like so many things in the Black experience, it goes back to slavery.

Consider...

On January 31, 1865 the 13th amendment to the constitution, abolishing slavery, was passed by Congress. It was then ratified, and officially became the law of the land on December 6, 1865. It is one of the most important and historic documents in American history.

But it contains a loophole...

That loophole is the "exception clause" in the amendment. The 13th amendment states that slavery and involuntary servitude are illegal *"except as a punishment for a crime."*

But that brief, seemingly insignificant clause, allowed the South to rebuild its economy after the Civil War, through prison labor. Black people were arrested in large numbers, often for very minor offenses, and thus deemed "criminals." "It was our nation's first prison boom," states Michele Alexander, author of "The New Jim Crow."

And the trend toward incarceration of Black people continued and expanded. There are three factors that have contributed to that expansion:

- The War on Drugs.
- The growth of for-profit prisons.
- The incarceration of people unable to provide their bail money.

These three factors have caused our prison populations to skyrocket. Though violent crime has been on the decline since 1980, the prison population has more than quadrupled.

In a recent speech to the national NAACP, President Obama said that, "Although the United States has only 5% of the world's population, it has 25% of the world's incarcerated people. And the United States has a rate of incarceration four times higher than China, and has more people incarcerated than the top 35 European nations combined!"

And most of them are Black.

According to Adam Gopnick in "The Caging of America," the incarceration rate for Black people is seven times what it is for whites.

How did this happen?

A political sea change occurred in the nineteen seventies when Nelson Rockefeller was Governor of New York. Though he had been in favor of drug rehabilitation earlier, he suddenly made an abrupt about-face. He held a press conference in January of 1973, launching a dramatic new campaign to toughen drug laws. He called for mandatory prison sentences of 15 years to life for drug dealers and addicts – even those caught with small amounts of marijuana, cocaine, and heroin.

And because Rockefeller's new drug campaign sounded so tough, and dramatic, it was enthusiastically embraced by other politicians like Nixon and Reagan. Rockefeller's program started a criminal justice revolution. It was a tsunami.

"The War on Drugs" has had a devastating effect on society, disproportionately affecting communities of color. Statistics show that white people and Black people use drugs on a roughly equal basis, but Black people are jailed on drug charges ten times more often than whites. As President Obama has commented, "This means that, at any one time, there are one million Black fathers behind bars. Fathers whose families need them. And most of them are non-violent drug users."

The War on Drugs has vastly increased the prison inmate population, and created a need for new prisons to house the additional inmates. It set the stage for the modern Prison-Industrial-Complex.

A number of new companies came into existence to take advantage of the new for-profit prison boom. Two of the largest and most financially successful have been the Correction Corporation of America (CCA), and GEO Group Inc. They are now both publicly traded stocks on the Stock Exchange. CCA's share price went from one dollar in 2000 to $34.34 in 2013. And in the last two decades, CCA's profits have increased by 500%

Wall Street banks are some of the biggest investors in the for-profit prison industry. Welles Fargo has around $100 million invested in GEO Group, and $6 million in CCA. Other major investors include Bank of America, Fidelity Investments, General Electric, and The Vanguard Group.

In 2011 the for-profit prison industry took in over $5 billion in revenue.

The bottom line of these businesses is very simple: the more people they can put in their prisons, the more money they make. Where prisons were once a necessary and legitimate part of the criminal justice system, they have now become a big, money-making opportunity, where investors can rake in millions.

...with devastating consequences for countless lives and families along the way.

What can we do?

The activity of a group of students from Columbia University offers a hopeful clue. In June 2013, they discovered that the University owned $8 million worth of CCA stock. The students formed a group called Columbia Prison Divest. They delivered a letter to the president of the University demanding total divestment from CCA, and full disclosure of future investments. And by June 2015, the board of trustees of Columbia University voted to divest from the private prison industry.

Drugs are not good for us, and can cause a lot of harm and personal disruption. We're all better off not taking them. But the War on Drugs, and it's off-spring, the for-profit prison industry, are both evil and sinful. They need to be stopped.

So what can we do?

Here are three places we can start:

- Engage in the political process to work to eliminate the War on Drugs. There is already movement in the direction of change in this area, but we need to be actively involved and intentional. This is politics at both the local and the national level.

• The strategy used by the Columbia University students in their activist organization, Columbia Prison Divest, offers an excellent template for the rest of us. If we have investments directly or indirectly in for-profit prison stocks, we can act to personally divest from them. Or, if we know of any other people or organizations that have these stocks in for-profit prisons, we can encourage them to divest. The harm that comes from for-profit prison businesses is far too great for them to continue unopposed.

• Finally, one of the big causes of incarceration in this country is lack of bail money due to poverty. One way to change this situation is through active engagement with the criminal justice system on the local level, to change the laws or the application of the laws. Still another strategy is to set up funds specifically designed to give bail money to people who have been picked up, but are unable to afford bail.

So, to return to our original question: "Is there justice in America?"

The answer is, No, there isn't justice in America. And there won't be until we all work together to bring about the huge changes our country so desperately needs.

XXX

CHAPTER 6

THE SECOND ASSASSINATION OF MARTIN LUTHER KING

Black History Month, every February, is a truly wonderful month. It provides an opportunity to look at American history through the prism of the Black experience. We discover the stories of Black people we've never heard of before, but whose work profoundly affects our lives every day. Did you know that blood transfusions and traffic lights were both invented by Black people?

But we also discover that some of the stories we thought we knew very well, are stories we only know in part. There are other chapters beyond the ones we already know.

Consider the story of the historic Voting Rights Act …

The passing of the Voting Rights Act in 1965 was one of our country's greatest achievements. It was designed to reverse America's long history of racial injustice and discrimination. This law provided the tools that finally gave Blacks the right to fully participate in the electoral process. President Reagan called The Voting Rights Act "the crown jewel of civil rights legislation."

The law was written to end not only existing voter discrimination, but also any new methods of voter disenfranchisement that might be created in the future. Any jurisdiction with a history of voter discrimination, was required by the Voting Rights Act to submit any proposed changes in their election laws for pre-clearance reviews by federal authorities. The jurisdictions needed to prove that their proposed changes were not going to be discriminatory.

That system remained intact for 48 years.

Then, in 2013, a case arising in Alabama, Shelby County vs. Holder, came to the Supreme Court. And in its ruling, the court struck down the long-standing pre-clearance review from the Voting Rights Act.

So, the crucial pre-clearance review of the Voting Rights Act, designed to protect and insure justice for all citizens, was obliterated by the Supreme Court.

It was the second assassination of Martin Luther King.

And, as in the past, Texas is once again at the forefront of efforts to keep people of color from full participation in the political process. In 2011, Texas passed a stringent law requiring voters to provide certain types of ID before they could vote. Initially this law was blocked by the Voting Rights Act pre-clearance procedures.

Then came the Supreme Court law eliminating the protection of the Voting Rights Act pre-clearance procedures. And within hours of the Supreme Court ruling, the Texas attorney general revived the 2011 voter ID law.

Without the protections of the Voting Rights Act, the Texas law sailed through, and is now the law of Texas, denying many Texas citizens the right to vote.

What kind of ID does the Texas law require in order to vote?

If you have a concealed-carry gun permit, that is considered ample identification to allow you to vote. However. If you are a student at one of the Texas State Universities, your school identification isn't considered sufficient identification to allow you to vote.

So, in Texas, you can vote if you carry a concealed weapon, but you can't vote if you're a university student!

The number of registered voters who are denied the right to vote because of this law is estimated to be more than 600,000. And, no big surprise, a large percentage of those people denied voting rights turn out to be Black and Latino.

The only way the Supreme Court ruling can be overturned now, at this point, is by an act of Congress. But so far there hasn't been any Republican co-sponsor for a Senate bill. And there hasn't yet been a hearing on any proposed bill that would restore what the Supreme Court destroyed.

The Voting Rights Act was one of the towering achievements of American history. It came about only because of the struggle, sacrifice and courage of activists and members of the Student Nonviolent Coordinating Committee, led by the visionary leadership of Rev. Dr. Martin Luther King Jr. And it was accomplished only after the heroism of March 7, 1965, "Bloody Sunday," and the voting rights marches from Selma to Montgomery that finally led to the passage of the act. The Voting Rights Act is foundational to our country as a democracy.

With the passage of the Voting Rights Act the United States took the decisive step toward making its frequently voiced ideals a reality.

But democracy is fragile.

With its 2013 decision. the Supreme Court has left the Voting Rights Act critically wounded. It is on life support.

The only way the Voting Rights Act can be restored is for Congress to take up, and pass, new amendments that will restore the Voting Rights Act to its full strength.

As citizens, we must demand this of Congress.

Unless every citizen has a full voice in our democracy, then nobody else's voice truly matters.

Without the full Voting Rights Act, we can't be the democracy we claim to be. We need to insist on the true restoration of each person's democratic voice.

We should demand nothing less.

XXX

CHAPTER 7

THE DECLARATION OF INDEPENDENCE, PART 2

In 1776, our country's founding fathers signed the Declaration of Independence. As the foundational document for our fledgling nation, the Declaration promised "liberty and justice for all."

Yet all of those original signers of the Declaration were slave holders. Even our first president, George Washington, was a slave holder.

And on May 21, 1793, a twenty-two-year-old woman named Ona Judge, one of Washington's slaves, escaped from Washington's mansion in Philadelphia and raced for freedom. Washington rounded up a posse, and they rode off to try to hunt her down and recapture her.

Ona Judge narrowly escaped the posse, and was never caught. But she was in constant danger, and for the rest of her years lived the perilous life of a hunted fugitive. Judge told her own personal story in interviews she gave to abolitionist newspapers in 1845 and 1847.

"Liberty and Justice for All?"

Yes, but not for the founding fathers' slaves...

The dissonance between our country's founding aspirations and its harsh racial inequities has sliced through American history like a Mason-Dixon line.

And there have been protests. First with Fredrick Douglas and John Brown in the 1870's. Then the protests of the Civil Rights Era and Rev. Dr. Martin Luther King. Later, the 1992 L.A. uprising, stemming from the Rodney King beating, along with the fiery justice sermons of Rev. Dr. Jeremiah Wright. And more recently the Black Lives Matter protests, along with Colin Kapaernick.

But just as there have been legitimate protests against racial injustice, there have been loud objections to those protests. Some of the loudest were in response to the sermons of Rev. Dr. Jeremiah Wright.

In the early days of President Obama's candidacy, Obama was linked with Jeremiah Wright, who had been his former pastor. Enemies of Obama found videos of Wright's sermons that seemed highly critical of this country and its government. The videos went viral on the internet. People accused Wright of being unpatriotic and anti-American.

But are Jeremiah Wright's fiery sermons really anti-American? Can a person criticize this country and its racial injustice, and still be a patriot?

I believe the answer is, yes.

Coincidentally, I have personally heard Rev. Wright preach about thirty different times. The video clips of Wright that flooded the internet were carefully cherry-picked to discredit Wright and Obama, and were each only a few seconds in length. But I happen to have heard thirty full-length sermons of Jeremiah Wright, delivered not on video, but in person.

It happened several years ago in Los Angeles. I've been going to a Black church for the last twenty-five years. I have also continued going to my original white church. It was at my Black church that I heard Jeremiah Wright. He is an absolutely spellbinding preacher!

Every year for several years, during Black History Month, the church would have a weeklong revival, with a powerhouse program and sermon every night. For several of those years Jeremiah Wright was the guest preacher.

There are two things that should be noted about Jeremiah Wright's worldview and his sermons. The first thing is that Jeremiah Wright has what he describes as an unapologetically "Afro-centric" view of the Bible. By this he means to call our attention to the fact that, since most of the events of the Bible, Old and New Testament, took place near the Equator, it's reasonable to suppose that many biblical characters were dark-skinned. It's interesting to note in this connection, that in Egyptian antiquities unearthed by archaeologists, many of the faces depicted are clearly Black people.

As a white person, I don't find this view of the Bible in any way jarring or heretical. In fact, at this point, having heard Jeremiah Wright around thirty times, I feel that his Afro-centrism has greatly deepened and enlarged my overall understanding of scripture. It geographically contextualizes it.

The other thing that is important to note about Jeremiah Wright is the nature of the audiences to whom he typically delivers his sermons (and hence the videos). Those audiences are almost always overwhelmingly Black. And the reality of Black people in America is very different from the reality of white people.

Many young Black men in this country feel unjustly under attack by the law and the police, because they are. The number of unarmed young Black men killed by police continues to steadily rise. The United States is a very dangerous, hostile country for Black people.

Has there been progress? Absolutely! And most Black people I know would readily agree with that. But consider the state of racism through an analogy with physical illness. A person can be seriously ill with cancer, experience a dramatic remission of symptoms, but still die from the disease.

For many Black people in America today, it's beginning to look as though our earlier progress toward a just and equitable society may just have been a temporary remission.

So, this is the context in which Jeremiah Wright has preached the vast majority of his sermons, and from which most of the YouTube videos were taken. He is a voice delivering a message of hope and encouragement to Black people, who are still suffering the ravages of a two-hundred-year siege of racism.

Is Jeremiah Wright critical of America? Yes. As he should be. And as **we** should be, if we are to be true patriots.

The Declaration of Independence? It is a utopian vision for our country where we offer "liberty and justice for all."

But the original Declaration of Independence is really just "The Declaration of Independence, Part 1", a ***document***, where we offer the vision of a utopian country with liberty and justice for all. What we need now is "The Declaration of Independence, Part 2," where we ***fulfill*** that earlier, utopian document.

It's like an architectural project. We begin with the plan, the blueprint, where we outline the wonderful building we plan to build. That's "The Declaration of Independence, Part 1."

Then there's the construction, the actual building we conceived in the earlier blueprint. That's "The Declaration of Independence, Part 2."

Now we need to build the building.

We owe it to Ona Judge.

XXX

CHAPTER 8

"WE HAVE MET THE ENEMY AND IT IS US"

It's been twenty-five years now, since I began going to a Black church on a regular basis, while continuing to go to my original white church. What an amazing adventure it has been, and continues to be!

What have I learned?

Basically, there are four things I have learned. Here they are:

ONE: The first thing I learned was how little I actually knew about the Black experience. I knew a number of individual Black people in different parts of my life, and thought I had a fairly good sense of what Black peoples' lives were like. But I came to understand how wrong I was. I really had no idea what their experience was like.

I think that's true of most white people.

Many white people I know, who would almost certainly consider themselves "liberals," know a Black person or two at work, or in some community organization. And, because they're friendly with that person, and have good relations with them, they assume therefore that they "know" the Black experience, and have some understanding of it.

Nothing could be farther from the truth.

Groups of white people, where whites are in the clear majority, hold subtle dangers for Black people. There may well be pockets of racial animosity, either hidden or unacknowledged, and Black people have learned to be acutely aware of them. In situations where white people predominate, Blacks are often reluctant to be too open.

So, would you like to find out about the real state of race relations in America today? Go to a place where Black people are in the majority. You'll find more truth there.

TWO: The second thing I learned was just how resistant many white people are to move outside their own socio-economic comfort zones. It's not so much a matter of racial hostility. I think it's more a reluctance on the part of many white people to do anything that might reflect on their own status.

When I first began my adventure/experiment of going to both a Black and a white church, a number of people in the white church were interested and enthusiastic.

At least for a while.

But as time went on, and I continued going to both churches, the attitudes at the white church began to change. It wasn't dramatic, but it was noticeable. I could see that people were uncomfortable with what I was doing. They didn't know what to make of it, or how to respond. I had stepped outside the acceptable boundary of things.

One night at a party of people from the white church, a woman pointedly said to me, "You're not coming back, are you?"

And she said this, even though I was still going to the white church! It's true I was now going to both churches, but I hadn't *abandoned* the white church; I was still going to it! I had just expanded the reach of my church and faith activities. But the way she said it, she made it sound as though I had somehow betrayed the white church.

Her attitude was one of puzzlement. It was as though she was saying, "We have a wonderful congregation of brilliant, successful people, a fabulous choir, and great preaching. What could you possibly hope to find anywhere else that we don't already have here?"

Actually, I have a great love for my white church. One Easter Sunday during the seventies, at a time when I was an atheist, and not open to going to church, I agreed to go to an Easter Sunday church service, at my wife Sally's urging. Not having any regular church home, I chose that church at random.

In the middle of the service, I had a powerful conversion experience. Six words came to me, that I knew were from God. The words were: "You belong here. Work it out."

I've been working it out ever since.

That church was the setting for my own personal Easter Sunday resurrection. And although I love it, and still go to it from time to time, it has come to feel like a socio-economic bubble. It is too self-contained for me; a gated community of the spirit.

Black people are acutely aware of the resistance white people feel about moving outside their socio-economic comfort zones.

I have a good friend who is a Black woman, and a minister. She told me that one of the most hurtful things in race relations for her came *after* integration. That's right, *after*.

At that point, the Jim Crow laws were gone, and there were no restrictions on what church a person could go to. Whites could go to a Black church, and Blacks could go to a white church.

But what actually happened was that a few Black people trickled into white churches, but virtually no white people ever ventured into Black churches. Even after "integration" it was still segregated!

My friend said she found this extremely hurtful. It was as though white people were saying, "You are welcome to come to our wonderful white church, but why in the world would we ever want to go to your Black church?"

The irony is that some of the most powerful and uplifting spiritual experiences I've ever had have been in the Black church.

THREE: The third thing I've learned from my experience in the Black church is the depth of need and pain that exists in the Black community. There have been enormous improvements in race relations in the last fifty years, but huge problems remain and some have grown larger.

The War on Drugs and the giant business of for-profit prisons have all come about since the great civil rights victories of the sixties. But both of these problems have had devastating effects on the Black community. And they were both problems I learned about through my involvement in my Black church.

And it was because of my involvement in my Black church that I first began to understand the true nature of racism in American society.

FOUR: The fourth thing I've learned from my time in the Black church, is how easy and joyful it can be to actually have that conversation about race that we need to have.

To use a familiar church structure or framework as the entry point into a new culture can be extremely effective, as I mentioned in Chapter One. And the guidelines I mentioned in Chapter One can insure that the experience will be successful. The key is to go in Love and Good Will. And go there frequently enough, and for a long enough period of time, that people can see you truly *are* going in Love and Good Will.

For me the experience has been joyful and life changing. I have gained many new friends in my Black church and they have blessed me hugely in many ways. And I believe those same blessings are available to anyone!

All you have to do is show up.

XXX

ABOUT THE AUTHOR

David Evans began his writing career in Cleveland, after college, writing funny greeting cards for American Greetings. He has written over 4,000 cards, including many bestsellers.

Later David moved to Los Angeles, where he worked as a comedy writer, winning an **EMMY Award** for writing on ***The Monkees***.

Drawing on his background as the son of a Presbyterian minister, he wrote **"THE GOOD BOOK...of Bible Cartoons,"** with drawings by long-time drawing partner Sherman Labby.

David has written about his spiritual journey in his book **"Does GOD Ever Speak Through CATS?"**

Another collaboration with drawing partner Sherman Labby is his graphic novel comedy adventure, **"The Hooper Brothers: Who's in Front?"**

In addition to humor, David is also an award-winning mediator. As part of his early mediation training David went to South Africa for a conflict resolution immersion experience, where he met with members of Archbishop Desmond Tutu's **Truth and Reconciliation Commission.**

For three years he served as a mediator for the **Los Angeles County Court Alternative Dispute Resolution Program**. At 16,000 cases a year it is the largest such program in the nation. For two of David's three years with the court, he won **"The Outstanding Case of the Year Award."**

He currently writes a blog for **Psychology Today**. The name of his blog is, **"Can't We All Just Get Along?"**

Made in the USA
Coppell, TX
23 December 2020

45190138R00031